No Turning Back:

Breaking Free from
the Grip of Yesterday

Self-Published by
Alisa L. Grace
Sanford, FL 32771

ISBN: 978-1-966129-50-9

First Edition

Printed in the United States of America

Library of Congress Cataloging-in-Publication Data
Grace, Alisa L.

Title of the Book: No Turning Back: Breaking Free from the Grip of Yesterday

Library of Congress Control Number: 2024925941

Disclaimer: The views expressed in this book are those of the author and do not necessarily reflect any organizations or individuals mentioned.

Acknowledgments: The author wishes to thank God, Her Husband (Linion), Victory Temple of God, Florida SPECS, Unity Youth Association, All About Serving You, Angels-ANJ Events, NordeVest, and Love & Create Life for their support and contributions.

This Book is Dedicated To

This book is dedicated to everyone who feels stuck in the shadows of their past—those held back by regret, nostalgia, fear, or even past successes.

To the dreamers who wonder if it's too late to start again, the weary who feel paralyzed by failure, and the hopeful who long to step into God's promises but aren't sure how—this book is for you.

May you find the courage to let go of what was, the faith to trust God with what is, and the boldness to embrace the abundant life He has prepared for you.

Above all, this book is dedicated to the glory of God, whose mercy makes all things new, whose love casts out fear, and whose grace calls us forward into lives of purpose and hope.

To Him be the glory, now and forever.

Why Read This Book?

Are you feeling stuck—replaying past mistakes, clinging to former successes, or held back by fear of the unknown? Do you long to move forward but feel trapped by the weight of "what was"? If so, this book is for you.

Inspired by the story of Lot's wife and supported by biblical wisdom, this book is a transformative guide to breaking free from the chains of the past and stepping boldly into the future God has prepared for you. Whether you're struggling with regret, nostalgia, or uncertainty, this book will help you realign your focus, deepen your faith, and take actionable steps toward growth and renewal.

"No Turning Back: Breaking Free from the Grip of Yesterday" is more than just a book—it's a call to action. Through relatable examples, practical insights, and a step-by-step guide rooted in Scripture, you'll discover how to release what's behind and embrace the abundant life God has for you.

What You Will Learn

1. **How to Trust God for the Future**

   ☐ Learn how faith transforms fear into hope and enables you to move forward confidently, even in the face of uncertainty.

2. **The Power of Letting Go**

   ☐ Understand how clinging to the past—whether successes or failures—can hinder your growth, and discover how to release these burdens to God.

3. **How to Renew Your Mind**

   ☐ Replace negative thought patterns with the truth of God's Word and develop a mindset aligned with His promises for your life.

4. **Building Forward Momentum**

   ☐ Discover how small, consistent steps of obedience can lead to significant breakthroughs and help you walk in your God-given purpose.

5. **The Rewards of Moving Forward**

   ☐ Explore the abundant blessings that come when you fully commit to God's plan and resist the temptation to look back.

6. **Practical Tools for Daily Transformation**

□ Engage with transformative questions, prayer prompts, and reflections that will guide you through your journey of faith and renewal.

This book will challenge, encourage, and inspire you to trust God more deeply and step boldly into the future He has prepared for you. By the end, you'll be equipped to leave the past behind, walk forward in faith, and embrace the life of purpose and blessing God has designed for you.

If you're ready to stop looking back and start moving forward, this book is the next step in your journey. Let's go—there's no turning back!

Contents

Introduction:
Why We Look Back

Scripture Reference:
"Do not call to mind the former things, or ponder things of the past." (Isaiah 43:18)

Life has a way of tempting us to stay stuck in the "what was." We replay memories of glory days, relive past victories, and rehearse stories of "the good old times." Some people build their identity entirely on who they used to be, never realizing that their fixation on the past keeps them from stepping into the future God has for them; like Lot's wife, they find themselves frozen—not literally as a pillar of salt, but emotionally and spiritually, unable to move forward.

Take the example of an ex-athlete who once dominated the court, the field, or the track. They were celebrated, admired, and envied. But now, years have passed. They spend their days recounting their high school championships or that one remarkable season, ignoring the reality that their life has stalled. Instead of using the discipline and lessons of their athletic career to mentor the next generation, they sit in bitterness, lamenting the loss of their prime. They're stuck in "used to be," blind to the possibilities of "what could be."

Or consider a former businessperson who once achieved financial success and status. Their name carried weight, their phone calls were always answered, and their influence seemed limitless. Now, faced with life's inevitable changes, they cling to stories of how prosperous they used to be. Rather than seeking new ways to grow or contribute, they live in nostalgia, paralyzed by the belief that their best days are behind them.

Nostalgia can feel comforting, even intoxicating, but it has a dark side. When we cling to the past, we lose sight of what God is doing now and what He promises for the future. Lot's wife serves as a cautionary tale for all of us. She had been given clear instructions: flee Sodom and do not look back. But as she was being rescued from destruction, she couldn't resist one last glance at the life she was leaving behind. That look cost her everything—her longing for what had robbed her of the new life God was giving her.

This book is about the transformative power of letting go. It's about recognizing that our glorious or painful past does not define our future. God has a plan for your life that requires you to move forward. As Isaiah 43:18 reminds us, we should not dwell on former things. God is doing something new, calling you to be part of it.

But moving forward isn't easy. Nostalgia and regret can grip our hearts and minds, making us believe that life will never be as good as it once was. For some, it's the allure of past successes; for others, it's the weight of past mistakes. Either way, living in the past keeps us from entering the future.

This book is your invitation to release yesterday's grip and embrace tomorrow's possibilities. It will help you understand how God's Word calls us to let go, move forward, and trust Him for what's ahead. We'll look at examples of biblical figures who overcame their pasts to fulfill their God-given purpose. You'll learn practical strategies to renew your mind, overcome regret, and take steps toward a future filled with hope and promise.

As you journey through these pages, ask yourself: What keeps me from moving forward? Are you holding on to former success, afraid you'll never achieve something greater? Are you trapped by regret, believing that your mistakes disqualify you from a better future? Whatever your "Sodom" might be, God calls you out. But to walk into His promises, you must resist the urge to look back.

Lot's wife looked back and became stuck. But you don't have to. You can choose to trust God, press forward, and step into the new things He has in store for you. Let's take this journey together, breaking free from the grip of yesterday and embracing the abundant life God has prepared for your future.

Chapter 1:
The Fate of Lot's Wife

Scripture Reference:
"But Lot's wife looked back, and she became a pillar of salt."
(Genesis 19:26)

The story of Lot's wife is a sobering reminder of the cost of looking back. God had extended His mercy to Lot's family, rescuing them from the destruction of Sodom. They were given one explicit instruction: *"Do not look back."* It was not a suggestion or a gentle warning but a command. Yet, in a moment of hesitation and longing, Lot's wife turned her gaze back toward the city she was leaving, and she became a pillar of salt.

Why did she look back? Perhaps it was the familiarity of Sodom, the comfort of her home, or the memories of a life she wasn't ready to let go of. Whatever the reason, her disobedience and attachment to the past cost her the future God was leading her toward.

Lot's wife represents all of us tempted to cling to what God has called us out of. Whether it's a toxic relationship, an unhealthy habit, a former lifestyle, or even a mindset of pride or self-reliance, we often struggle to let go of the familiar—even when it's destructive. Her fate teaches us that looking back can immobilize us, making us spiritually stagnant and unable to embrace the life God has prepared for us.

God doesn't lead us out of places to harm us; He leads us out to protect and guide us into something better. When we disobey and look back, we essentially say, "God, I don't trust You to take me somewhere better than where I've been." This lack of trust leads to spiritual paralysis, just as Lot's wife became physically frozen as a pillar of salt.

Transformative Questions:

1. What are the "Sodom" areas in your life—places, habits, or relationships—that God calls you to leave behind?

_____

_____

_____

_____

2. What fears or attachments are causing you to hesitate in trusting God's plan for your future?

_____

_____

_____

_____

3. How would your life change if you fully embraced God's call to move forward without looking back?

_____

_____

_____

_____

Reflection: The Cost of Looking Back

Looking back is more than a glance over the shoulder—it's a sign of divided loyalty. Lot's wife was leaving behind a city and a way of life. She longed for what God had already judged unworthy, and that longing made her incapable of fully receiving God's mercy.

Consider what you might be holding onto. Are you clinging to past successes, unwilling to step into the unknown? Are you dwelling on failures, unable to forgive yourself, or trust that God has a better plan? Whatever your "Sodom" might be, know that God's call to move forward is for your good. He wants to take you to a place of healing, purpose, and abundance—but you must be willing to leave the past behind.

_____

_____

_____

_____

_____

_____

_____

_____

_____

_____

_____

_____

_____

_____

Prayer Prompt: Moving Forward Without Looking Back

Heavenly Father,

I thank You for Your mercy and the ways You are leading me out of the places that no longer serve me. Forgive me for when I've hesitated, doubted, or looked back. Help me trust Your plans for my life, knowing they are good and filled with hope. Show me the areas of my life that I need to release into Your hands, and give me the courage to walk forward without hesitation. Lord, I choose today to turn my focus to You and the future You have for me. In Jesus' name, Amen.

Key Takeaway:

The story of Lot's wife reminds us that looking back can cost us everything. God's plans require trust, obedience, and a forward focus. He is calling you to release the past and step boldly into the promises He has prepared. Will you trust Him enough not to look back?

Chapter 2:
God's Call to Move Forward

Scripture Reference:

"Forget the former things; do not dwell on the past. See, I am doing a new thing! Now it springs up; do you not perceive it?"
(Isaiah 43:18-19)

God is a forward-moving God. From the beginning of creation to fulfilling Christ's mission, God's plans have always been about progression, growth, and renewal. Yet, as humans, we often resist the call to move forward. The unknown can feel intimidating, and the comfort of what we know—good or bad—can make us hesitant to embrace the future.

In Isaiah 43, God reminds His people not to dwell on the past because He is doing something new. Imagine if Abraham had refused to leave his homeland when God called him or if the Israelites had chosen to stay in Egypt because the wilderness seemed too daunting. These pivotal moments required faith, trust, and a willingness to let go of the past.

The same is true for us today. God calls each of us to move forward into the plans He has prepared, but we cannot fully step into His purpose while clinging to the past. Whether it's fear of the unknown, attachment to what was, or shame from previous mistakes, we often hold onto what God has already asked us to release.

It's always for our good when God calls us to move forward. His plans are not to harm us but to prosper us (Jeremiah 29:11). Like a gardener pruning a plant, God removes what is no longer fruitful so that new growth can emerge. Our job is to trust Him in the process and take the steps of faith necessary to follow where He leads.

Transformative Questions:

1. What areas of your life is God asking you to leave behind so He can lead you into something new?

   _____

   _____

   _____

   _____

2. What fears or doubts are keeping you from stepping forward in faith?

   _____

   _____

   _____

   _____

3. How can you actively trust God to guide your steps into the future He has planned for you?

   _____

   _____

   _____

   _____

Reflection: Trusting the God of New Beginnings

God's call to move forward is always accompanied by His provision and presence. Just as He provided manna in the wilderness for the Israelites and led them by a pillar of cloud and fire, He promises to guide and sustain you as you step into new territory. Reflect on areas of your life where you may be resisting change. What new thing might God be trying to do in your life? What blessings could you be missing because you're holding onto the past?

Faith isn't about knowing every step of the journey—it's about trusting the One who leads. Remember, God's plans for you are greater than anything you could imagine. The same God who created the universe is the One calling you forward. Trust Him to write the next chapter of your story.

_____

_____

_____

_____

_____

_____

_____

_____

_____

_____

_____

Prayer Prompt: Trusting God's Call to Move Forward

Heavenly Father,

Thank You for being a God who always moves us forward. I have sometimes hesitated to embrace the future because of fear, doubt, or attachment to the past. Help me to trust Your plans for my life and to release anything that holds me back from Your purpose. Open my eyes to perceive the new thing You are doing, and give me the courage to follow wherever You lead. I choose to walk by faith today, trusting that Your plans for me are good. In Jesus' name, Amen.

Key Takeaway:

God's call to move forward is an invitation to trust Him and embrace the new things He is doing in your life. By releasing the past, you open yourself to His blessings, purpose, and provision. Will you take the step of faith and trust the God who always makes all things new?

Chapter 3:
Overcoming the
Trap of Past Glory

Scripture Reference:

"The glory of this present house will be greater than the glory of the former house." (Haggai 2:9)

There's a subtle danger in reminiscing about past successes. While celebrating victories and achievements is essential, dwelling on them can create a trap that keeps us from embracing God's greater plans for us. Past glory, if idolized, becomes an anchor instead of a stepping stone.

Consider those who live their lives recounting "the good old days." Perhaps it's the former athlete who once broke records but now spends every moment talking about what they accomplished instead of mentoring others or pursuing new goals. Or the successful businessperson whose best years feel like they are behind them. Instead of seeking God for the next chapter, they remain stuck, mourning the past and missing the opportunities in the present.

Even in the Bible, we see individuals who faced the temptation to glorify the past. When the temple in Jerusalem was being rebuilt, some of the older Israelites wept because the new temple didn't appear as grand as Solomon's. They were so focused on the splendor of the past that they couldn't recognize the greater spiritual glory God was preparing for the future (Haggai 2:9).

When we focus on past glory, we miss God's ability to do something new. What if your most outstanding achievements are not behind you but ahead of you? What if God wants to use your past success as a foundation for something even more incredible? Clinging to the past limits our ability to see the "new thing" God is doing (Isaiah 43:19).

Transformative Questions:

1. Are there past successes or moments of glory that you've elevated to a place of idolization, making it difficult to move forward?

_____

_____

_____

_____

2. How can you honor what God has done in your life without allowing it to keep you from embracing what He's doing now?

_____

_____

_____

_____

3. What steps can you take today to trust that the best is yet to come, even if it looks different than what you've experienced before?

_____

_____

_____

_____

Reflection: Releasing Yesterday's Victories

Letting go of past glory doesn't mean forgetting or dishonoring what God has done in your life. Instead, it's about releasing your grip on the past so you can embrace the future. Ask yourself: Are you still depending on yesterday's accomplishments for your sense of worth or significance? God wants to remind you that your value isn't tied to what you've done but to who you are in Him.

The same God who enabled your victories in the past is still with you today. He isn't finished with you. Your best days are not necessarily your most celebrated moments—when you trust God enough to step into His new plans for your life.

Prayer Prompt: Trusting God for Greater Things

Heavenly Father,

Thank You for the victories and achievements of my past. I honor the ways You have blessed and guided me, but release them into Your hands. Help me not to cling to what was but to trust You for what will be. Open my eyes to see the new opportunities You are placing before me, and give me the courage to pursue them with faith. You are doing something new in my life, and I trust that my best days are ahead. In Jesus' name, Amen.

Key Takeaway:

While past glory can be a source of encouragement, it is not a destination. God is always calling us forward, promising that the glory of the future will surpass the achievements of the past. Will you trust Him to take you higher and farther than you've ever been before?

Chapter 4:
Breaking Free from Regret

Scripture Reference:

"Brothers and sisters, I do not consider myself yet to have taken hold of it. But one thing I do: Forgetting what is behind and straining toward what is ahead, I press on toward the goal to win the prize for which God has called me heavenward in Christ Jesus." (Philippians 3:13-14)

Regret can be a heavy chain, binding us to mistakes, failures, and missed opportunities. It whispers lies that our errors define us and that we are disqualified from God's plans. Regret can blind us to the beauty of grace and keep us anchored in a past that God has already redeemed.

Peter's story is one of the most profound examples of breaking free from regret. After denying Jesus three times, Peter was consumed by shame. He wept bitterly, likely replaying his failure in his mind repeatedly. But Jesus, in His infinite mercy, didn't leave Peter in that place of regret. After His resurrection, Jesus lovingly restored Peter, reminding him that his calling was still valid (John 21:15-17).

Regret paralyzes us by making us believe that our past mistakes are greater than God's ability to forgive and restore. This is a lie. The Apostle Paul, who once persecuted Christians, could have lived in perpetual regret for his actions. Instead, he focused on God's grace and the mission ahead. In Philippians 3, Paul makes it clear that he was not perfect but determined to forget what was behind him and press forward.

What about you? Does regret trap you? Do you replay the same painful memories, wondering if you could ever be forgiven or valuable again? The truth is that God's grace is greater than your most significant failure. He wants to take your regret and turn it into a testimony of His redemption.

Transformative Questions:

1. Are there mistakes or failures from your past that you are strug-
    gling to forgive yourself for?

    _____

    _____

    _____

    _____

2. How can you begin to see your past failures through God's grace
    rather than your guilt?

    _____

    _____

    _____

    _____

3. What steps can you take to press forward into the future God
    has for you, leaving regret behind?

    _____

    _____

    _____

    _____

Reflection: Releasing Regret to Receive Restoration

Regret can be an influential teacher when it leads us to repentance, but it becomes a prison when it keeps us stuck in shame. God has already forgiven you for your mistakes, so why are you still holding onto them? Imagine Peter if he had chosen to stay in regret rather than accept Jesus' restoration. He would have missed the opportunity to lead the early church and become a pillar of the faith.

Your failures are not the end of your story. God calls you to release regret, accept His forgiveness, and walk boldly into your purpose. Regret reminds us that we are human, but grace reminds us that we are loved, forgiven, and redeemed.

_____

_____

_____

_____

_____

_____

_____

_____

_____

_____

_____

_____

Prayer Prompt: Releasing Regret and Embracing Grace

Heavenly Father,

Thank You for the gift of grace that covers my mistakes and failures. I confess that I have been holding onto regret, replaying moments You have already forgiven. Help me to see myself through Your eyes—not as a prisoner of my past, but as a recipient of Your mercy. I now release my regrets to You and ask for the strength to move forward. Thank You for loving me and restoring me. I trust that You will use my past for Your glory and my future for Your purpose. In Jesus' name, Amen.

Key Takeaway:

Regret doesn't have to define your story. God's grace is bigger than your failures, and His plan for your life is still intact. Choose to release regret, embrace His forgiveness, and press forward into the future He has prepared for you. Will you trust Him to turn your past mistakes into a testimony of His redemption?

Chapter 5:
Faith for the Future

Scripture Reference:

"Now faith is confidence in what we hope for and assurance about what we do not see." (Hebrews 11:1)

Faith is the foundation of moving forward. Without it, the unknown future can feel overwhelming, even paralyzing. Faith allows us to trust that God's promises will come to pass even when we can't see how they unfold. The Bible is filled with stories of men and women who stepped into the unknown, trusting that God would guide and provide for them.

Consider Noah, who built an ark obeying God's instructions even though the rain had not yet fallen. Or Abraham, who left everything familiar to journey to a land God would show him. These acts of faith were not blind leaps but confident steps taken in response to God's Word.

Faith in the future requires surrendering control. It means believing God's plans are better than ours, even when we can't see the whole picture. It's not about ignoring challenges but trusting that God will equip us to face them. Faith transforms fear into hope and uncertainty into anticipation.

Transformative Questions:

1. What specific fears or uncertainties are holding you back from trusting God with your future?

   _____

   _____

   _____

   _____

2. How has God shown His faithfulness in the past, and how can that strengthen your faith now?

   _____

   _____

   _____

   _____

3. What steps can you take today to demonstrate your faith in God's promises?

   _____

   _____

   _____

   _____

Reflection: Embracing the Unknown with Confidence

Faith is not the absence of doubt but the decision to trust God in the midst of it. Reflect on areas where you may hesitate to step forward because you're waiting for clarity or guarantees. God doesn't ask us to understand every detail; He asks us to trust Him. Just as He guided Noah, Abraham, and countless others, He will guide you, too.

_____

_____

_____

_____

_____

_____

_____

_____

_____

_____

_____

_____

_____

_____

_____

_____

_____

_____

Prayer Prompt: Strengthening Faith for the Future

Heavenly Father,

Thank You for being faithful in every season of my life. Help me to trust You with my future, even when I can't see the full path ahead. Strengthen my faith and remind me of Your promises. Teach me to walk confidently in the assurance that You are always with me. I release my fears to You and choose to move forward in faith. In Jesus' name, Amen.

Key Takeaway:

Faith is the key to embracing the future. By trusting God's promises, you can confidently step forward, knowing He will guide and provide for every step of the journey.

Chapter 6:
Developing a New Mindset

Scripture Reference:

"Do not conform to the pattern of this world, but be transformed by the renewing of your mind." (Romans 12:2)

Your mindset shapes your reality. If you're stuck in patterns of thinking rooted in the past, it's nearly impossible to move forward into the future God has for you. Developing a new mindset is essential for embracing change and walking in the fullness of God's promises.

The Bible emphasizes the importance of renewing our minds. We cannot achieve this transformation on our own—it requires the Holy Spirit and intentional engagement with God's Word. By replacing old, limiting thoughts with the truth of Scripture, we align our thinking with God's plans.

The Apostle Paul exemplifies a transformed mindset. Once a persecutor of Christians, Paul became one of the most influential figures in the early church. His mindset shift allowed him to see himself not as a sinner condemned by his past but as a new creation in Christ. This same transformation is available to you.

Transformative Questions:

1. What thought patterns or beliefs prevent you from fully trusting God's plans?

   _____

   _____

   _____

   _____

2. How can you replace negative or limiting thoughts with truths from Scripture?

   _____

   _____

   _____

   _____

3. What practical steps can you take to renew your mind daily?

   _____

   _____

   _____

   _____

Reflection: Choosing Transformation Over Conformity

Renewing your mind requires intentional effort. Reflect on the areas where you may conform to worldly thinking patterns rather than embracing God's truth. How can you shift your focus from "what was" to "what God is doing"?

_____

_____

_____

_____

_____

_____

_____

_____

_____

_____

_____

_____

_____

_____

_____

_____

_____

_____

Prayer Prompt: Renewing My Mind

Heavenly Father,

my mind. Teach me to align my thinking with Your Word and to release any beliefs that don't reflect Your truth. Transform me from the inside out to fully embrace Your plans for my life. I trust You to guide my thoughts and lead me to a new way of thinking. In Jesus' name, Amen.

Key Takeaway:

Developing a new mindset allows you to see yourself and your future through God's eyes. By renewing your mind, you can break free from limiting beliefs and walk confidently into God's plans.

Chapter 7:
Building Forward Momentum

Scripture Reference:

"The steps of a good man are ordered by the Lord, and He delights in his way." (Psalm 37:23)

Faith requires action. Once you decide to move forward, the next step is building momentum. Forward momentum is about small, consistent steps of obedience that align with God's direction.

Imagine a river flowing toward the ocean. The water doesn't arrive at its destination in one giant leap but through steady, persistent movement. In the same way, building momentum in your spiritual journey requires daily decisions to trust God and take the next step, no matter how small.

The Bible offers countless examples of people who built forward momentum through obedience. David didn't become king overnight—years of preparation and faithfulness in small tasks, like tending sheep and defeating Goliath, paved the way. Likewise, your small steps of faith will lead to significant breakthroughs.

Transformative Questions:

1. What small steps of obedience can you take today to build momentum in your spiritual journey?

_____

_____

_____

_____

2. How can you remain faithful in the "small things" while trusting God for the "big things"?

_____

_____

_____

_____

3. What does it look like to trust God to order your steps in this season of life?

_____

_____

_____

_____

Reflection: Trusting the Process

Momentum doesn't happen overnight, but every step you take matters. Reflect on areas where you've hesitated to act because you don't see immediate results. How can you trust God to use your tiny, faithful steps to create forward momentum in your life?

_____
_____
_____
_____
_____
_____
_____
_____
_____
_____
_____
_____
_____
_____
_____
_____
_____
_____
_____

Prayer Prompt: Building Forward Momentum

Heavenly Father,

Thank You for ordering my steps and guiding my path. Help me to be faithful in the small things as I trust You for the big things. Teach me to follow consistent obedience steps, even when the results aren't immediate. I believe that You are working in every moment and that my forward momentum is part of Your greater plan. In Jesus' name, Amen.

Key Takeaway:

Momentum is built through small, consistent steps of obedience. Trust God to guide your journey, and know that every step forward is part of His grander plan for your life.

Chapter 8:
The Rewards of
Not Looking Back

Scripture Reference:

"No one who puts a hand to the plow and looks back is fit for service in the kingdom of God." (Luke 9:62)

Obedience to God's call comes with great rewards. When you choose not to look back, you open yourself to the abundant blessings God has in store for your future. Letting go of the past frees your hands to receive what God is giving you now.

Jesus' words in Luke 9:62 are a call to commitment. Looking back is not just a distraction—it's a sign of divided loyalty. God's kingdom requires us to move forward with an undivided heart, fully committed to His purpose.

The Bible contains examples of people who experienced God's rewards because they chose not to look back. The Israelites entered the Promised Land, Paul finished his race, and Peter became a pillar of the early church—all because they trusted God and stayed focused on His promises.

Transformative Questions:

1. What rewards might you be missing because you are still looking back?

   _____

   _____

   _____

   _____

2. How can you fully commit to God's purpose for your life without hesitation or regret?

   _____

   _____

   _____

   _____

3. What steps can you take to embrace the blessings and opportunities God is offering you now?

   _____

   _____

   _____

   _____

Reflection: Staying Focused on God's Promises

Looking back keeps us from experiencing the fullness of God's blessings. Reflect on areas where you may hesitate to let go of the past. What opportunities and rewards might God have waiting for you if you fully commit to His call?

_____

_____

_____

_____

_____

_____

_____

_____

_____

_____

_____

_____

_____

_____

_____

_____

_____

_____

Prayer Prompt: Embracing God's Rewards

Heavenly Father,

Thank You for the blessings and rewards You have prepared for me. Help me to let go of the past and stay focused on Your promises. Teach me to trust that what You have ahead is far greater than anything I've left behind. I fully commit my heart, mind, and future to You. In Jesus' name, Amen.

Key Takeaway:

The rewards of not looking back are immeasurable. By fully committing to God's call, you position yourself to receive His abundant blessings and experience the fullness of His purpose for your life. Will you trust Him enough to press forward without hesitation?

Conclusion:
Moving Forward in Faith

As you've journeyed through these chapters, you've seen the dangers of looking back and the transformative power of trusting God with your future. From Lot's wife, who was paralyzed by longing for the past, to Peter, Paul, and others who chose to embrace God's call forward, the Bible consistently shows us the rewards of faith, obedience, and a forward-focused mindset.

Faith in the future is the foundation of moving forward. It's not about having all the answers or guarantees but about trusting that God's promises are true and His plans are good. Developing a new mindset aligns your thoughts with God's Word, enabling you to see yourself and your circumstances through His eyes. Building momentum through daily, faithful steps of obedience while fully committing to God's call ensures you receive the abundant blessings He has prepared for you.

Reflection: A Life Fully Committed to God's Call

Think about your own journey. What has God been calling you to release? Are there areas of your life where you're still clinging to the past—whether through regret, nostalgia, or fear? Are you ready to let go and fully commit to the future God has for you? The rewards of moving forward far outweigh the comfort of staying where you are.

God invites you to experience something greater: a future filled with purpose, hope, and abundant grace. But to step into that future, you must trust Him completely and leave the past behind.

Call to Action: A Step Forward

1. **Take Inventory of Your Life:** Reflect on the areas where you may be stuck—whether it's regret, fear, or attachment to past success. Write these down and prayerfully surrender them to God.

2. **Set a Faith-Filled Goal:** Identify one area where God calls you to step forward. This could be a new opportunity, a step of obedience, or a renewed mindset.

3. **Commit to Daily Action:** Build momentum forward by taking small, consistent daily steps. This could mean praying, studying Scripture, or actively pursuing the next step in God's plan for you.

4. **Trust God for the Results:** Remember that you don't have to figure everything out. Faith is about trusting God with what you can't see and believing that He will guide and provide as you move forward.

Prayer Prompt: A Prayer of Commitment

Heavenly Father,

Thank You for the lessons You've taught me through this journey. I release the past to You—my regrets, fears, and successes. I surrender my future into Your hands, trusting that Your plans for me are good. Help me take steps of faith each day, renewing my mind and building momentum. Strengthen my heart to remain focused on Your promises and fully commit to Your purpose for my life. I trust You to lead, guide, and bless me as I progress. In Jesus' name, Amen.

Key Takeaway:

Your future is filled with purpose, hope, and blessing in God's hands. Trust Him enough to let go of the past, embrace a new mindset, and step boldly into His plans for you. **The time to move forward is now. Will you take the first step?**

30-Day Challenge Title

"Forward in Faith:
A 30-Day Challenge to Step Into God's Promises"

Introduction Letter

Dear Friend,

Congratulations on saying yes to this 30-day journey of transformation! **"Forward in Faith"** is more than just a challenge—it's an intentional commitment to step into the fullness of God's promises for your life. Over the next 30 days, we'll dive deep into Scripture, engage in transformative reflection, and build a habit of prayer to help you let go of the past and walk boldly into the future God has prepared for you.

This challenge is designed for anyone who feels stuck—whether in regret, fear, or even nostalgia for past successes. With God's Word as our foundation, we'll explore themes like faith, mindset renewal, obedience, and embracing the "new thing" God is doing. Each day, you'll receive a Scripture, a transformative question, and a prayer prompt to guide your heart and mind.

My prayer for you during this challenge is that you'll grow in confidence, deepen your faith, and find the courage to trust God's plans for your future. Remember, transformation doesn't happen all at once—it's a journey of small, faithful steps. You're not alone in this; God is with you every step of the way, and I'm cheering for you too.

Let's step forward in faith together!

With love and encouragement,

Your Sister In Christ

30-Day Challenge: "Forward in Faith"

Week 1: Faith as the Foundation

Day 1:

Scripture: Hebrews 11:1 – *"Now faith is confidence in what we hope for and assurance about what we do not see."*

Transformative Question: What area of your life is God asking you to trust Him with, even though you can't see the outcome?

_____

_____

_____

_____

_____

_____

_____

_____

_____

_____

_____

_____

_____

_____

Prayer Prompt: Lord, help me to trust You with the unseen parts of my life. Strengthen my faith as I take steps forward.

Day 2:

Scripture: *Proverbs 3:5-6 – "Trust in the Lord with all your heart and lean not on your own understanding."*

Transformative Question: Where have you relied on your understanding instead of trusting God?

_____

_____

_____

_____

_____

_____

_____

_____

_____

_____

_____

_____

_____

_____

_____

_____

_____

_____

_____

Prayer Prompt: Father, I surrender my understanding to You. Teach me to trust in Your ways above my own.

Day 3: Trusting God in the Unknown

Scripture: *"The Lord is my shepherd; I lack nothing. He makes me lie down in green pastures, He leads me beside quiet waters, He refreshes my soul. He guides me along the right paths for His name's sake." (Psalm 23:1-3)*

Transformative Question: Are you allowing God to guide you, or are you trying to control the direction of your life?

_____

_____

_____

_____

_____

_____

_____

_____

_____

_____

_____

_____

_____

_____

Prayer Prompt: I trust You to guide me along the right paths. Help me to let go of my desire for control and trust in Your perfect plan.

Day 4: Releasing Fear to Embrace Faith

Scripture: *"For God has not given us a spirit of fear, but of power and of love and of a sound mind." (2 Timothy 1:7)*

Transformative Question: What fears are holding you back from stepping into the future God has for you?

_____

_____

_____

_____

_____

_____

_____

_____

_____

_____

_____

_____

_____

_____

_____

Prayer Prompt: Father, I release my fears to You. Fill me with Your power, love, and peace, and help me to walk forward in faith.

Day 5: Faithful in the Small Things

Scripture: *"Whoever can be trusted with very little can also be trusted with much." (Luke 16:10)*

Transformative Question: How can you practice faithfulness in the small tasks God has given you today?

_____

_____

_____

_____

_____

_____

_____

_____

_____

_____

_____

_____

_____

_____

_____

Prayer Prompt: Lord, teach me to value the small things and to be faithful in every task You place before me. My obedience to the little things will prepare me for greater things ahead.

Day 6: Fixing Your Eyes on Jesus

Scripture: *"Let us fix our eyes on Jesus, the author, and perfecter of our faith, who for the joy set before Him endured the cross." (Hebrews 12:2)*

Transformative Question: Where are you fixing your focus? Are your eyes on Jesus or on your circumstances?

_____

_____

_____

_____

_____

_____

_____

_____

_____

_____

_____

_____

_____

_____

_____

_____

Prayer Prompt: Jesus, help me to fix my eyes on You. When distractions come, remind me to keep my focus on Your promises and faithfulness.

Day 7: God is Your Rock

Scripture: *"Truly He is my rock and my salvation; He is my fortress, I will not be shaken." (Psalm 62:6)*

Transformative Question: How can trust in God as your rock and fortress give you the confidence to step into the unknown?

_____

_____

_____

_____

_____

_____

_____

_____

_____

_____

_____

_____

_____

_____

_____

Prayer Prompt: Father, thank You for being my rock and my refuge. Help me to stand firm in Your strength and trust that You will keep me steady as I move forward.

Letter of Encouragement for Week 1:

"Well, Begun is Half Done!"

Dear Friend,

You've completed your first week! I'm so proud of you for committing to this journey of faith. Each day, you're taking steps to trust God more fully. Remember, faith is like a seed—it takes time to grow. Keep nurturing it with God's Word and prayer, and you'll begin to see the fruits of transformation. You've got this!

Week 2: Renewing the Mind

Day 8:

Scripture: Romans 12:2 – "Do not conform to the pattern of this world, but be transformed by the renewing of your mind."

Transformative Question: What negative thought patterns prevent you from embracing God's truth?

_____

_____

_____

_____

_____

_____

_____

_____

_____

_____

_____

_____

_____

_____

_____

_____

Prayer Prompt: Lord, renew my mind today. Replace my doubts and fears with Your truth and promises.

Day 9:

Scripture: 2 Corinthians 10:5 – "We take captive every thought to make it obedient to Christ."

Transformative Question: How can you align your thoughts with God's truth today?

_____

_____

_____

_____

_____

_____

_____

_____

_____

_____

_____

_____

_____

_____

_____

_____

Prayer Prompt: Father, help me to take captive every thought that doesn't align with Your Word. Transform my thinking by Your Spirit.

Day 10: Replacing Lies with Truth

Scripture: *"Then you will know the truth, and the truth will set you free." (John 8:32)*

Transformative Question: Are there lies you've believed about yourself or your circumstances that need to be replaced with God's truth?

_____

_____

_____

_____

_____

_____

_____

_____

_____

_____

_____

_____

_____

Prayer Prompt: Lord, help me identify any lies I've believed. Replace them with the truth of Your Word, and set me free from anything that holds me back.

Day 11: Thinking on What is Good

Scripture: *"Finally, brothers and sisters, whatever is true, whatever is noble, whatever is right, whatever is pure, whatever is lovely, whatever is admirable—if anything is excellent or praiseworthy—think about such things."*
(Philippians 4:8)

Transformative Question: Are your thoughts aligned with what is good, pure, and admirable, or are you dwelling on negativity?

_____

_____

_____

_____

_____

_____

_____

_____

_____

_____

_____

_____

Prayer Prompt: Father, teach me to focus my thoughts on what is good and praiseworthy. Help me to fill my mind with things that honor You and bring peace.

Day 12: Guarding Your Mind

Scripture: *"Above all else, guard your heart, for everything you do flows from it." (Proverbs 4:23)*

Transformative Question: How can you protect your mind and heart from negativity or influences that distract you from God's truth?

_____

_____

_____

_____

_____

_____

_____

_____

_____

_____

_____

_____

_____

_____

_____

Prayer Prompt: Lord, help me to guard my heart and mind. Show me how to protect myself from thoughts or influences that pull me away from You.

Day 13: Taking Thoughts Captive

Scripture: *"We demolish arguments and every pretension that sets itself up against the knowledge of God, and we take captive every thought to make it obedient to Christ." (2 Corinthians 10:5)*

Transformative Question: How can you take your thoughts captive today and make them obedient to Christ?

_____

_____

_____

_____

_____

_____

_____

_____

_____

_____

_____

_____

_____

_____

_____

_____

Prayer Prompt: Father, give me the strength to control my thoughts. Teach me to align every thought with Your truth.

Day 14: The Power of Gratitude

Scripture: *"Give thanks in all circumstances; for this is God's will for you in Christ Jesus." (1 Thessalonians 5:18)*

Transformative Question: How can a heart of gratitude shift your perspective and renew your mind today?

_____

_____

_____

_____

_____

_____

_____

_____

_____

_____

_____

_____

_____

_____

_____

_____

_____

Prayer Prompt: Lord, thank You for all the blessings You've given me. Help me to cultivate a heart of gratitude and to focus on Your goodness in every situation.

Letter of Encouragement for Week 2: "Keep Going—Renewal is Happening!"

Dear Friend,

You've completed the second week of the **"Forward in Faith"** challenge! This week, you've focused on renewing your mind, replacing lies with truth, and guarding your thoughts. I hope you've begun to experience the freedom and peace that comes from aligning your thinking with God's Word.

Transformation doesn't happen overnight, but you're taking steps that bring you closer to God's purpose for your life every day. Keep pressing forward, trusting that God is working in you and through you. You're doing amazing!

With love and encouragement,

Your Sister In Christ

Week 3:
Building Forward Momentum

Day 15:

Scripture: *Psalm 37:23 – "The steps of a good man are ordered by the Lord."*

Transformative Question: What small, faithful step can you take today toward the future God is calling you to?

_____

_____

_____

_____

_____

_____

_____

_____

_____

_____

_____

_____

_____

_____

_____

_____

Prayer Prompt: Father, order my steps today. Help me to take small, faithful actions that align with Your will.

Day 16:

Scripture: *Philippians 3:13-14 – "Forgetting what is behind and straining toward what is ahead."*

Transformative Question: What is one thing you need to release to embrace what God has ahead fully?

_____

_____

_____

_____

_____

_____

_____

_____

_____

_____

_____

_____

_____

_____

_____

_____

_____

Prayer Prompt: Lord, I release what's holding me back. Help me to strain toward the future You have for me.

Day 17: Moving by Faith, Not by Sight

Scripture: *"For we live by faith, not by sight." (2 Corinthians 5:7)*

Transformative Question: Are you waiting to see every detail before moving forward, or are you trusting God to lead the way?

_____
_____
_____
_____
_____
_____
_____
_____
_____
_____
_____
_____
_____
_____
_____
_____

Prayer Prompt: Lord, help me to walk by faith and not by sight. Teach me to trust that even when I can't see the path, You are guiding me every step of the way.

Day 18: Persevering Through the Process

Scripture: *"Let us not become weary in doing good, for at the proper time we will reap a harvest if we do not give up."*
(Galatians 6:9)

Transformative Question: How can you stay faithful and persevere, even when progress feels slow?

_____

_____

_____

_____

_____

_____

_____

_____

_____

_____

_____

_____

_____

Prayer Prompt: Father, give me the strength to persevere. Help me to trust that my faithfulness today will produce a harvest in Your perfect timing.

Day 19: Trusting the Work God is Doing in You

Scripture: *"Being confident of this, that He who began a good work in you will carry it on to completion until the day of Christ Jesus." (Philippians 1:6)*

Transformative Question: How can you trust that God is working in you, even when you don't see immediate results?

_____

_____

_____

_____

_____

_____

_____

_____

_____

_____

_____

_____

_____

_____

Prayer Prompt: I trust that You are at work in my life. Help me to be patient and confident that You will complete the good work You've started in me.

Day 20: Embracing Your Calling

Scripture: *"For we are God's handiwork, created in Christ Jesus to do good works, which God prepared in advance for us to do." (Ephesians 2:10)*

Transformative Question: What is one step you can take today to walk in the purpose God has prepared for you?

_____

_____

_____

_____

_____

_____

_____

_____

_____

_____

_____

_____

_____

_____

_____

_____

Prayer Prompt: Father, thank You for creating me with a purpose. Help me to walk boldly in the calling You've placed on my life, trusting that You've prepared the way.

Day 21: Trusting God to Make Your Steps Firm

Scripture: *"The Lord makes firm the steps of the one who delights in Him; though he may stumble, he will not fall, for the Lord upholds him with His hand." (Psalm 37:23-24)*

Transformative Question: Do you trust God to firm your steps, even when the journey is uncertain?

_____

_____

_____

_____

_____

_____

_____

_____

_____

_____

_____

_____

_____

_____

Prayer Prompt: I delight in You and trust You to guide my steps. Even when I stumble, I know You are holding me up. Help me to walk forward with confidence in Your strength.

Letter of Encouragement for Week 3: "You're Building Momentum!"

Dear Friend,

You've completed Week 3 of the **"Forward in Faith"** challenge! This week, you focused on building momentum, persevering through challenges, and trusting God with every step. It's not always easy to keep moving forward, but you're doing it—and I'm so proud of you!

Each small step you've taken is part of God's bigger plan for your life. Keep trusting Him, even when the journey feels slow or uncertain. He's guiding, strengthening, and preparing you for what's ahead. Momentum is building, and God's purpose for your life is unfolding. Keep going—you're closer than you think!

With love and encouragement,

Your Sister In Love

Week 4:
The Rewards of Moving Forward

Day 22:

Scripture: *Luke 9:62 – "No one who puts a hand to the plow and looks back is fit for service in the kingdom of God."*

Transformative Question: What blessings could you be missing by looking back instead of moving forward?

_____

_____

_____

_____

_____

_____

_____

_____

_____

_____

_____

_____

_____

_____

_____

_____

_____

Prayer Prompt: Father, help me to stay focused on the future You have for me. Let me not look back, but press on in faith.

Day 23:

Scripture: *Haggai 2:9 – "The glory of this present house will be greater than the glory of the former house."*

Transformative Question: How can you trust that God's future blessings will surpass your past experiences?

_____

_____

_____

_____

_____

_____

_____

_____

_____

_____

_____

_____

_____

_____

_____

_____

Prayer Prompt: I trust You to bring greater glory and blessings in my future than anything I've experienced before.

Week 4: Days 24-30

Day 24: Trusting in God's Timing

Scripture: *"There is a time for everything and a season for every activity under the heavens." (Ecclesiastes 3:1)*

Transformative Question: Are you trusting God's timing or trying to rush His plans for your life?

_____

_____

_____

_____

_____

_____

_____

_____

_____

_____

_____

_____

_____

_____

_____

Prayer Prompt: Heavenly Father, help me to trust Your perfect timing. Teach me to wait patiently and faithfully for the blessings and opportunities You have prepared for me.

Day 25: Walking in Obedience

Scripture: *"If you are willing and obedient, you will eat the good things of the land." (Isaiah 1:19)*

Transformative Question: What area of your life is God asking you to be more obedient in so that you can receive His blessings?

_____

_____

_____

_____

_____

_____

_____

_____

_____

_____

_____

_____

_____

_____

_____

_____

Prayer Prompt: Lord, show me how I can walk in obedience today. Help me to trust that Your commands are for my good and lead to abundance in my life.

Day 26: Pressing Through Challenges

Scripture: *"Consider it pure joy, my brothers and sisters, whenever you face trials of many kinds because you know that the testing of your faith produces perseverance." (James 1:2-3)*

Transformative Question: How can you view your current challenges as opportunities for growth and perseverance?

_____

_____

_____

_____

_____

_____

_____

_____

_____

_____

_____

_____

_____

_____

Prayer Prompt: Father, help me to see my challenges through Your eyes. Teach me to trust that every trial shapes me for the future You've prepared.

Day 27: Embracing God's Abundance

Scripture: *"The thief comes only to steal and kill and destroy; I have come that they may have life, and have it to the full." (John 10:10)*

Transformative Question: Are you ready to fully embrace the abundant life God has promised you?

_____

_____

_____

_____

_____

_____

_____

_____

_____

_____

_____

_____

_____

_____

_____

Prayer Prompt: Lord, I thank You for the promise of abundance. Help me to walk boldly in the fullness of life that You offer through Christ.

Day 28: Remaining Faithful in the Small Things

Scripture: *"Whoever can be trusted with very little can also be trusted with much." (Luke 16:10)*

Transformative Question: How can you remain faithful in the small tasks God has placed before you as He prepares you for greater responsibilities?

_____

_____

_____

_____

_____

_____

_____

_____

_____

_____

_____

_____

_____

_____

Prayer Prompt: Heavenly Father, help me see the value of the small things. Teach me to be faithful and diligent in everything You've entrusted to me.

Day 29: Staying Focused on the Prize

Scripture: *"I press on toward the goal to win the prize for which God has called me heavenward in Christ Jesus."*
(Philippians 3:14)

Transformative Question: What distractions do you need to let go of to stay focused on God's calling for your life?

_____

_____

_____

_____

_____

_____

_____

_____

_____

_____

_____

_____

_____

_____

_____

_____

Prayer Prompt: Lord, keep my eyes fixed on You and the goal You've set before me. Help me to let go of anything that pulls me away from Your purpose.

Day 30: Trusting the God Who Holds Your Future

Scripture: *"For I know the plans I have for you, declares the Lord, plans to prosper you and not to harm you, plans to give you hope and a future." (Jeremiah 29:11)*

Transformative Question: How can you trust God more fully with your future, knowing that He has plans to give you hope and prosperity?

_____

_____

_____

_____

_____

_____

_____

_____

_____

_____

_____

_____

_____

Prayer Prompt: Heavenly Father, thank You for holding my future in Your hands. I surrender every worry, fear, and uncertainty to You, trusting that Your plans for me are good.

Letter of Encouragement for Week 4: "You Did It!"

Dear Friend,

You've completed the **"Forward in Faith"** challenge! What an incredible accomplishment. Over the past 30 days, you've trusted God, renewed your mind, taken steps forward, and embraced His promises. You've let go of the past and chosen to move into the future with faith and confidence.

But this is not the end—it's a beginning. Every step you've taken has prepared you for the journey ahead. Keep building on this foundation. Trust God daily, stay in His Word, and continue taking small, faithful steps toward His purpose for your life.

I'm so proud of you, and know God is, too. He sees your heart and your commitment. As you move forward, remember that He is always with you, guiding and providing every step of the way.

You did it! Celebrate this moment, and let it inspire you to keep walking forward in faith.

With love and encouragement,

Your Sister In Christ

Post-Challenge Letter: Call to Action

Dear Friend,

Congratulations on completing the **"Forward in Faith"** challenge! Over the past 30 days, you've intentionally grown in faith, renewed your mind, and trusted God with your future. This journey has been about more than just letting go of the past—it's been about embracing the abundant life God has for you.

Now that the challenge is over, it's time to live out what you've learned. Here's your call to action:

1. **Stay in the Word:** Continue to spend time in Scripture daily. God's Word is your foundation for growth and transformation.

2. **Keep Building Momentum:** Don't stop taking small, faithful steps. Every step forward brings you closer to God's purpose for your life.

3. **Encourage Others:** Share your journey with someone else. Invite them to take the challenge or simply walk alongside them in faith.

Remember, transformation is a daily process. You've already made incredible progress, and God isn't finished with you yet. Keep moving forward, trusting Him to guide you every step.

I'm cheering and praying for you as you continue this faith journey. You've got this—and most importantly, God's got you.

With love and encouragement,

Your Sister In Christ

Additional Resources: Books to Support Your Journey

As you embark on the journey of moving forward and embracing the future God has for you, reading Scripture alongside books by trusted Christian authors can deepen your understanding and inspire your faith. Below is a curated list of resources to complement your reading of the Bible, which remains the primary and ultimate source of wisdom and truth.

How to Use This Resource

Start with daily Bible reading and meditation on the Scriptures listed above.

Select one or two books from the list to dive deeper into specific themes such as faith, renewing the mind, or embracing God's purpose.

As you read, journal your thoughts and prayers, noting insights and how they apply to your life.

Pray before and after reading, asking the Holy Spirit to guide you in understanding and applying the lessons.

Let these resources inspire and encourage you as you walk forward in faith, trusting God for what lies ahead!

The Primary Source

1. **The Bible**

   - Start with these sections:

     - *Genesis 18-19*: The story of Lot and his wife.

     - *Isaiah 43:18-19*: God's promise to do a new thing.

     - *Philippians 3:12-14*: Pressing on toward the goal.

     - *Hebrews 11*: Examples of faith.

     - *Romans 12:2*: Renewing your mind.

Recommended Books

2. **"The Purpose Driven Life" by Rick Warren**

   - Discover your God-given purpose and learn how to live with eternal significance.

3. **"Battlefield of the Mind" by Joyce Meyer**

   - Understand the importance of renewing your mind and how to overcome negative thought patterns.

4. **"The Bait of Satan" by John Bevere**

   - Learn how to release offenses, let go of the past, and live free from unforgiveness.

5. **"It's Not Supposed to Be This Way" by Lysa TerKeurst**

   - Gain perspective on how God can turn disappointments into divine appointments.

6. **"Crazy Faith" by Michael Todd**

   - A powerful guide to stepping out in bold faith and trusting God in the unknown.

7. **"Don't Give the Enemy a Seat at Your Table" by Louie Giglio**

   - Practical insights into reclaiming your focus, thoughts, and peace from the enemy's lies.

8. **"Unshakeable Trust" by Joyce Meyer**

- Learn how to trust God in every area of your life, especially when circumstances seem uncertain.

9. "Forgotten God" by Francis Chan

- Reconnect with the power and presence of the Holy Spirit to guide you into God's will.

10. "Your Best Life Now" by Joel Osteen

- Insights into living a fulfilled life by focusing on God's promises and potential for you.

Faith-Building Classics

11. "Mere Christianity" by C.S. Lewis

- A foundational Christian book exploring what it means to live out your faith.

12. "The Pursuit of God" by A.W. Tozer

- A timeless work calling readers to deepen their relationship with God.

13. "Experiencing God" by Henry Blackaby and Claude V. King

- A guide to recognizing and participating in God's work in your life.

14. "Streams in the Desert" by L.B. Cowman

- A devotional offering encouragement and wisdom for those in challenging seasons.

15. "The Practice of the Presence of God" by Brother Lawrence

- A short but powerful book on living every moment in God's presence.

Meet The Author

Alisa Ladawn Grace is an inspiring author, educator, and life coach who is passionate about helping individuals experience true transformation through faith and intentional living. With a Specialist Degree in Curriculum and Instruction and years of experience as a school administrator and nonprofit leader, Alisa combines her expertise in education with her deep spiritual insight to guide readers on a journey of growth, healing, and renewal.

Her latest book, *No Turning Back: Breaking Free from the Grip of Yesterday*, offers a powerful guide to letting go of past hurts, failures, and limitations to embrace a life of freedom and purpose. Through heartfelt stories, biblical truths, and practical strategies, Alisa empowers readers to overcome the chains of yesterday and step into the future God has planned for them. This book is an invitation to break free, trust God's promises, and live a life of peace and fulfillment.

Before *No Turning Back*, Alisa authored *Renewed: The Transformational Power of Putting Off the Old and Putting On the New*, a deeply impactful book inspired by Ephesians 4:22-24. In *Renewed*, Alisa leads readers through a journey of spiritual renewal, encouraging them to let go of old habits and embrace Christ-like virtues that bring lasting change and joy.

Alisa's writing reflects her mission to help people unlock their full potential—spiritually, emotionally, and practically. Her other works, including *Spirit Empowered: Living a Life of Grace, Com-*

passion, and Forgiveness and *Unlocking Your Great Potential*, inspire readers to cultivate kindness, forgiveness, and faith while overcoming life's challenges with resilience and hope.

Through her books, coaching, and leadership, Alisa Ladawn Grace offers a roadmap for those seeking to live fully in God's love and purpose. Her heartfelt and empowering message continues to impact lives, encouraging readers to let go of the past, embrace renewal, and walk boldly into the future with faith and confidence.